June 2012

HIGHWAY PROJECTS

Some Federal and State Practices to Expedite Completion Show Promise

GAO

Accountability ★ Integrity ★ Reliability

June 2012

GAO
Accountability * Integrity * Reliability

Highlights

Highlights of GAO-12-593, a report to congressional requesters

HIGHWAY PROJECTS

Some Federal and State Practices to Expedite Completion Show Promise

Why GAO Did This Study

Projects to construct, improve, and repair roads and bridges are fundamental to meeting the nation's mobility needs. However, completing highway projects—which generally involves four phases consisting of (1) planning, (2) preliminary design and environmental review, (3) final design and right-of-way acquisition, and (4) construction—can sometimes take a long time. In 2005, SAFETEA-LU established provisions to help expedite highway projects, including streamlining some portions of the environmental review process, allowing states to assume greater environmental review responsibilities under certain conditions, and establishing efforts that permitted delegation of some authority from the federal government to states. GAO was asked to (1) describe the process and factors that could affect highway project time frames, (2) examine state DOTs' views on the benefits and challenges of the provisions to expedite highway projects established in SAFETEA-LU, and (3) describe additional initiatives that state DOTs and FHWA have implemented to expedite the completion of highway projects. GAO surveyed officials from 52 state DOTs, including all states, the District of Columbia, and Puerto Rico; interviewed officials at FHWA, state DOTs, and federal resource agencies (agencies tasked with protecting natural, historic, or cultural resources); and analyzed legislation, regulations, and other reports and publications. U.S. DOT provided technical comments on a draft of this report, which GAO incorporated as appropriate.

View GAO-12-593. To view an e-supplement with more data see GAO-12-637SP. For more information, contact David J.Wise at (202) 512-2834 or wised@gao.gov.

What GAO Found

The process to complete highway projects is complicated and lengthy due to multiple factors. Specifically, highway projects can involve many stakeholders, including agencies at all levels of government, nongovernmental organizations, and the public. These stakeholders perform a number of tasks—for major highway projects, as many as 200 steps from planning to construction—but their level of involvement varies. For example, resource agencies like the U.S. Army Corps of Engineers or the U.S. Fish and Wildlife Service generally only become involved in a highway project if it affects the environmental or cultural resources that agency is tasked with protecting. Additional factors can lengthen project time frames, including the availability of funding, changes in a state's transportation priorities, public opposition, or litigation.

State departments of transportation (DOT) that GAO surveyed generally agreed that the provisions meant to help expedite highway projects established in the Safe, Accountable, Flexible, Efficient Transportation Equity Act: A Legacy for Users (SAFETEA-LU) could decrease time frames but found some provisions more useful than others. They most frequently agreed that the provision allowing for the use of protected public land—if such use has minor impacts on the property and is approved by relevant resource agencies—has the potential to save time and has few challenges to implementation. State DOTs reported that the other SAFETEA-LU provisions GAO studied have both potential benefits and challenges but, in some cases, they identified alternative solutions that could better serve their needs. For example, although respondents indicated that they could save time by implementing the issue resolution process established in SAFETEA-LU, they also noted that the use of written agreements between highway project stakeholders—such as federal resource agencies—could better serve their purposes. Survey respondents also indicated that they are generally not interested in implementing two SAFETEA-LU provisions that would delegate environmental review decision-making authority from the Federal Highway Administration (FHWA) to states, primarily because the states did not want to accept federal court jurisdiction for the decisions made under those provisions.

States have implemented a variety of efforts to expedite highway projects and FHWA has initiated efforts to expedite projects by sharing innovative practices. For example, in 1997, the North Carolina DOT implemented a project development process that promotes early involvement of highway stakeholders and reduces permit processing times from years to months. Other state efforts are more recent, prompted by streamlining concepts promoted by FHWA beginning in 2010 under an effort known as Every Day Counts. Through Every Day Counts, FHWA encouraged states to consider implementing 15 specific innovative practices during 2011 and 2012, including 13 practices that could help expedite highway project completion. FHWA plans to introduce a new set of initiatives during 2012 for implementation during 2013 and 2014. FHWA developed performance measures for Every Day Counts and is currently collecting data to determine if these initiatives have had a positive impact on expediting highway projects.

_____ United States Government Accountability Office

Contents

Abbreviations

AASHTO	American Association of State Highway and Transportation Officials
CE	categorical exclusion
DOT	department of transportation
EA	environmental assessment
EIS	environmental impact statement
FHWA	Federal Highway Administration
FWS	U.S. Fish and Wildlife Service
MPO	metropolitan planning organization
NEPA	National Environmental Policy Act of 1969
NGO	nongovernmental organization
SAFETEA-LU	Safe, Accountable, Flexible, Efficient Transportation Equity Act: A Legacy for Users
USACE	U.S. Army Corps of Engineers

View GAO-12-637SP Key Components

Highway Projects: Survey of State Departments of Transportation (GAO-12-637SP), an e-supplement to GAO-12-593.

United States Government Accountability Office
Washington, DC 20548

June 6, 2012

The Honorable Nick J. Rahall, II
Ranking Member
Committee on Transportation and Infrastructure
House of Representatives

The Honorable Peter A. DeFazio
Ranking Member
Subcommittee on Highways and Transit
Committee on Transportation and Infrastructure
House of Representatives

Projects to construct, improve, and repair roads and bridges are fundamental to meeting the nation's mobility needs. However, major federally funded highway projects can take a long time to complete. In 2005, the Safe, Accountable, Flexible, Efficient Transportation Equity Act: A Legacy for Users (SAFETEA-LU) established a number of provisions to help expedite the completion of highway projects, including streamlining some portions of the environmental review process, allowing states to assume greater environmental review responsibilities under certain conditions, and establishing pilot programs that permitted delegation of some authority from the federal government to states.

You requested that we report on the process associated with completing highway projects, as well as the impact of the SAFETEA-LU provisions meant to help expedite that process. Accordingly, this report (1) describes the process for planning, designing, and constructing federally funded highway projects and the factors that could affect project time frames; (2) presents state departments of transportation (DOT) views on the benefits and challenges of implementing provisions to expedite highway projects established by SAFETEA-LU; and (3) describes the additional initiatives that state DOTs and the Federal Highway Administration (FHWA) have implemented to expedite highway projects.

To describe the process for completing highway projects, as well as the factors that could affect project time frames, we reviewed and analyzed relevant legislation—particularly SAFETEA-LU—regulations, congressional hearing statements, and other reports and publications. To collect information on practices involved in the highway project process, as well as factors that could affect time frames, we conducted interviews with officials from (1) FHWA; (2) federal resource agencies, that is agencies tasked with protecting natural, historic, or cultural resources, such as the U.S. Army Corps of Engineers (USACE) or the U.S. Fish and Wildlife Service (FWS); and six state DOTs—Alaska, California, Missouri, North Carolina, Pennsylvania, and Utah—which were selected using a number of criteria, including participation in certain SAFETEA-LU provisions and geographic locations. These interviews are not generalizable to all states. To identify state DOT perspectives on the benefits and challenges associated with implementing SAFETEA-LU provisions meant to help expedite highway projects, we conducted a survey of 52 state DOTs, including all states, the District of Columbia, and Puerto Rico. We identified key provisions of SAFETEA-LU that were meant to help expedite highway projects, drafted the survey, pretested it with five state DOTs, and incorporated comments from external officials, including FHWA and the American Association of State Highway and Transportation Officials (AASHTO). Our response rate was 100 percent. More information on our survey can be found in appendix I, as well as in a separate e-supplement, GAO-12-637SP. To describe the practices state DOTs and FHWA have implemented on their own to help expedite highway projects, we included a series of questions in our survey of state DOTs asking respondents to identify such practices. We also conducted interviews with state DOTs and FHWA and analyzed responses from these entities.

We conducted this performance audit from June 2011 to June 2012 in accordance with generally accepted government auditing standards. Those standards require that we plan and perform the audit to obtain sufficient, appropriate evidence to provide a reasonable basis for our findings and conclusions based on our audit objectives. We believe that the evidence obtained provides a reasonable basis for our findings and conclusions based on our audit objectives. For more information on our scope and methodology, see appendix I.

Background

FHWA plays a key role in funding and overseeing the completion of highway projects. In addition to providing financial assistance and establishing standards for state DOTs to build and improve highways and roads, FHWA—through its division office in each state—provides technical expertise and fulfills oversight functions. State and local governments execute the programs by matching and distributing federal funds; planning, selecting, and supervising projects; and complying with federal requirements.

Funding for highway projects represents a large federal investment—about $39 billion in fiscal year 2011. Federally funded highway projects are typically developed in the following four phases:

1. *Planning.* State DOTs and metropolitan planning organizations (MPO) assess the need for a project in relation to other potential highway project needs.

2. *Preliminary design and environmental review.* State DOTs identify potential transportation solutions based on needs identified during planning, potential environmental and social effects of those solutions, project cost, and construction location; analyze the effect, if any, of the proposed project and potential alternatives on the environment; and select the preferred alternative.

3. *Final design and right-of-way acquisition.* State DOTs finalize design plans, acquire property, and relocate residents and businesses.

4. *Construction.* State DOTs award construction contracts, oversee construction, and accept the completed project.

In the preliminary design and environmental review phase, many activities are carried out pursuant to the National Environmental Policy Act of 1969 (NEPA) and other federal laws. Under NEPA, federal agencies must assess the effects of major federal actions—those they propose to fund, carry out or permit—that significantly affect the environment. NEPA has two principal purposes: (1) to ensure that an agency carefully considers detailed information concerning significant environmental impacts and (2) to ensure that this information will be made available to the public. NEPA generally requires federal agencies to prepare documentation showing the extent of the project's environmental impacts. Per NEPA, the lead agencies—usually a state DOT and FHWA—will determine which of the three documentation types is needed as follows:

- Projects referred to as 'categorical exclusions' (CE) are determined to not individually or cumulatively have a significant effect on the quality of the environment. These projects require no or limited environmental review or documentation under NEPA. Examples of highway projects that are generally processed as CEs include resurfacing, constructing bicycle lanes, installing noise barriers, and landscaping. The vast majority of highway projects are processed as CEs (see fig. 1). Based on data collected in 2009, FHWA estimates that approximately 96 percent of highway projects were processed as CEs.

Figure 1: Federal Highway Projects by NEPA Action Class

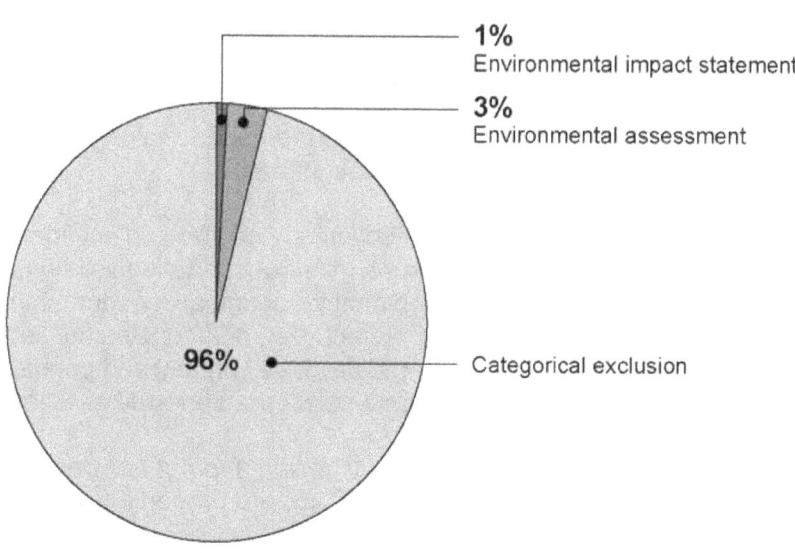

1%
Environmental impact statement

3%
Environmental assessment

96%

Categorical exclusion

Source: GAO analysis of 2009 FHWA data.

- An environmental impact statement (EIS) is required for proposed projects that are determined to have a significant effect on the environment. In broad terms, FHWA starts the EIS process by publishing a notice of intent in the *Federal Register*. It then consults with resource agencies—such as USACE or FWS—and solicits comments from the public on a draft EIS, incorporates comments into a final EIS, and issues a record of decision. Among other things, the record of decision—which is the final step for agencies in the EIS process—identifies (1) the decision made; (2) the alternatives considered during the development of the EIS, including the environmentally preferred alternative; and (3) plans to mitigate environmental impacts. For the 32 projects in which FHWA was the lead agency and signed the EIS in fiscal year 2009, the average amount of time from signing the notice of intent to signing the record of decision was 83 months—almost 7 years.[1] As noted, FHWA estimates that based on its 2009 data approximately 1 percent of all federal-aid highway projects in the United States were processed with

---

[1]For the 30 projects in which FHWA was the lead agency and signed the EIS in fiscal year 2010, the average amount of time from signing the notice of intent to signing the record of decision was 69 months.

GAO-12-593 Highway Projects

an EIS. While projects requiring an EIS are a small portion of all highway projects, they are likely to be high-profile, complex, and expensive projects. For these reasons, many efforts to expedite highway projects and reports which study those efforts, including this report, tend to focus on highway projects requiring an EIS.

- Project sponsors prepare an environmental assessment (EA) when it is not clear whether a project will have significant environmental impacts. An EA is intended to be a concise document that, among other things, briefly provides sufficient evidence and analysis for determining whether to prepare an EIS. If during the development of an EA, the project sponsor determines that the project will cause significant environmental impacts, the project sponsor will stop producing the EA and, instead, produce an EIS. However, an EA typically results in a finding of no significant impact, a document that presents the reasons why the agency has concluded that there are no significant environmental impacts to occur when the project is implemented. FHWA estimates that, based on its 2009 data, about 3 percent of all federal-aid highway projects were processed using an EA.

Numerous federal, state, and local laws determine the processes and tasks highway projects are to complete throughout the four phases. For example, SAFETEA-LU contains provisions that establish policies related to transportation planning and the environmental review process. Various environmental laws—including NEPA, the Endangered Species Act, the Clean Water Act, and the National Historic Preservation Act—establish processes and environmental requirements that projects must meet. Right-of-way acquisition must be accomplished according to the requirements of the Uniform Relocation Assistance and Real Property Acquisition Policies Act of 1970, as amended, a law designed to provide fair treatment of property owners and tenants when they are displaced by federally funded programs, including the construction of a federal-aid highway. Federal-aid highway projects are typically subject to a number of federally required contract provisions, such as nondiscrimination, payment of a predetermined minimum wage, and accident prevention. There are also numerous state and local laws—for example, several states, including California and North Carolina, have laws roughly equivalent to the federal NEPA—that projects must comply with and which help guide projects through various tasks in the process.

In addition, a number of provisions created by SAFETEA-LU are intended to help expedite highway projects. We analyzed seven of those provisions that have been implemented (see table 1), focusing primarily on those in

Title VI of SAFETEA-LU, which deals with transportation planning and project delivery.[2] We surveyed officials from 52 state DOTs about the potential benefits and challenges associated with each of these SAFETEA-LU provisions and did not ask states to quantify these benefits or challenges. During survey pretesting, we learned that any number of variables could impact the time frames for completing a project, such as the SAFETEA-LU provisions we were asking about in our survey, the complexity of each highway project, or even the personalities of individuals working on tasks for the project. As such, our survey findings generally do not indicate specific values for the benefits and challenges (such as time savings) from implementing or using the SAFETEA-LU provisions, but rather represent state DOTs' perspectives (i.e., the degree to which they agree or disagree that a particular factor could be a benefit or a challenge) on the potential benefits and challenges of those provisions.

---

[2]An additional provision that we reviewed—SAFETEA-LU Section 6003 "State assumption of responsibilities for certain programs and projects," codified at 23 U.S.C. § 325—has not yet been implemented. Numerical results from our survey on all the SAFETEA-LU provisions we studied, as well as more information on how we conducted our survey can be found in appendix I or in a separate e-supplement, GAO-12-637SP.

Table 1: SAFETEA-LU Provisions Meant to Help Expedite Highway Projects

GAO term[a]	SAFETEA-LU full title	Description	U.S. Code citation	SAFETEA-LU section
180-Day Statute of Limitations	Limitations on claims	Bars claims seeking judicial review of a permit, license, or approval issued by a federal agency for highway projects unless they are filed within 180 days after publication of a notice in the *Federal Register* announcing the final agency action, unless a shorter time is specified in the federal law under which the judicial review is allowed.	23 U.S.C. § 139(l)	6002
Categorical Exclusion Approval Authority	State assumption of responsibility for categorical exclusions	Authorizes U.S. DOT to assign and a state to assume responsibility for determining whether certain projects can be categorically excluded from the NEPA process.	23 U.S.C. § 326	6004
Design-Build Contracting[b]	Design build	Repealed the minimum cost requirements for use of design-build contracting for federal-aid highway projects. Also required the Secretary of Transportation to make changes to the design-build regulations, generally to permit a state transportation department to release requests for proposals and award design-build contracts prior to the completion of the NEPA process; however, it also precludes a contractor from proceeding with final design or construction before completion of the NEPA process.	23 U.S.C. § 112(b)(3)	1503(2)
Issue Resolution Process	Issue identification and resolution	Established procedures to resolve issues between state DOTs and relevant resource agencies.	23 U.S.C. § 139(h)	6002
Minor Impacts to Protected Public Land	Parks, recreation areas, wildlife and waterfowl refuges, and historic sites	Authorizes an historic site or publicly owned land from a park, recreation area, or wildlife or waterfowl refuge to be used for a transportation program or project if it is determined that such use would result in "de minimis impacts" to that resource.	23 U.S.C. § 138(b)	6009
NEPA Approval Authority	Surface transportation project delivery pilot program	Allows no more than five states to assume many federal environmental review responsibilities, in addition to determining whether certain projects can be categorically excluded from the NEPA process.	23 U.S.C. § 327	6005
Offering Financial Assistance to Stakeholder Agencies	Assistance to affected state and federal agencies	Allows a state to use its federal highway funds to support a federal or state agency participating in the environmental review process.	23 U.S.C. § 139(j)	6002

Source: Pub. L. No. 109-59.

[a]For purposes of this report, we have established terms for the SAFETEA-LU provisions we reviewed.

[b]Design-build contracting is a contracting method that combines the responsibilities for designing and constructing a project in a single contract instead of the more traditional approach of separating these responsibilities.

The Process to Complete Highway Projects Is Complex and Lengthy Due to Multiple Factors

Completing a highway project can involve many stakeholders—including federal, state, and local government agencies; nongovernmental organizations (NGO); and private citizens—and, for major highway projects, as many as 200 steps from planning through construction (see fig. 2). A number of additional factors can also affect project time frames.

Figure 2: Potential Stakeholders and Typical Steps Involved in a Major New Highway Project

Planning	Preliminary design and environmental review	Final design and right-of-way acquisition	Construction

	Planning	Preliminary design and environmental review	Final design and right-of-way acquisition	Construction
Potential stake-holders involved	State DOTs and Federal Highway Administration generally involved in all aspects of highway projects			
	• Local governments (such as metropolitan planning organizations or rural planning organizations)	• Federal resource agencies (such as U.S. Army Corps of Engineers for projects impacting wetlands, or U.S. Fish and Wildlife Service for projects impacting threatened and endangered plant and animal species) • State resource agencies (such as the state historic preservation office for projects impacting historic property) • Local governments • Nongovernmental organizations • Contractors • Private citizens	• Federal resource agencies • State resource agencies • Contractors • Private citizens	• State resource agencies • Contractors
Typical steps	• Assess transportation purpose and need • Solicit public comment • Gain approval to be included in the state's 20 year plan • Gain approval to be included in the state's short-term program (at least 4 years) for projects that are to be implemented, with expectation that funds will be available • Determine sources of funding	• Consider alignment issues and required lanes • Identify alternatives, including not building the project, to minimize potential harm to the environment and historic sites • Select preferred alternative • Prepare a preliminary design of the highway • Solicit comments on the project and its potential effects from private citizens and from local governments • Gain concurrence from federal agencies from which environmental and historic preservation concurrence is required	• Finalize design plans • Appraise and acquire property • Relocate utilities and affected citizens before construction, if necessary • Finalize project cost estimates	• Advertise and evaluate bids; award contracts • Begin construction • Resolve unexpected problems • Accept delivery

Source: GAO.

Wide Range of Stakeholders

A wide range of stakeholders can be involved in highway projects, from federal, state, and local agencies with varying missions and responsibilities to NGOs, contractors, and private citizens. Different factors, however, will help determine the extent to which stakeholders will become involved in the project. For example, if a highway project will not affect endangered or threatened species, it is likely that FWS—which is responsible for implementing the Endangered Species Act for freshwater and terrestrial species—will not become involved in the project. Additionally, some states have developed written agreements—known by a number of terms, including programmatic agreements or memoranda of agreement—with other state or federal agencies that can help to establish a process for consultation, review, and compliance with one or more federal laws, allowing for the project to be reviewed more quickly. Regardless, there are a host of stakeholders that could become involved in a highway project as follows:

- *Transportation agencies.* Federal and state transportation agencies are responsible for improving, maintaining, and planning highway systems with a focus on safety, reliability, effectiveness, and sustainability. Among other things, FHWA oversees planning and project completion by reviewing statewide long-range transportation plans, evaluating whether a project meets environmental protection requirements, and authorizing acquisition of property for highway projects it funds. State DOTs are typically the focal point for project planning and construction and are responsible for setting the relevant goals for the state, planning safe and efficient transportation, designing most projects, identifying and mitigating environmental impacts, acquiring property for highway projects, and awarding and overseeing construction contracts.

- *Federal resource agencies.* Federal resource agencies, such as those described below, are responsible for managing and protecting natural and cultural resources like wetlands, historic properties, forests, and wildlife:

  - *The Advisory Council on Historic Preservation*, established by the National Historic Preservation Act of 1966, seeks to promote the preservation, enhancement, and sustainable use of the nation's historic resources. The council advises the President and the Congress on national historic preservation policies and ensures federal agencies take such issues into account when developing and implementing federal projects.

  - *USACE* issues permits for the dredging and filling of waters of the United States, including wetlands within the agency's jurisdiction, under Section 404 of the Clean Water Act.

- *The Environmental Protection Agency* administers, among other things, the Clean Air and Clean Water Acts.

- *FWS* implements the Endangered Species Act with respect to freshwater and terrestrial species.

- *The National Marine Fisheries Service* implements, among other things, the Marine Mammal Protection Act and the Endangered Species Act with respect to most marine species and anadromous fishes (which spend portions of their life cycle in both fresh and salt water).

- *The U.S. Forest Service* transfers land for highway rights of way within the National Forest System to states through FHWA.

- *State resource agencies.* These state-level agencies are generally responsible for managing and protecting the state's natural and cultural resources.

  - State resource agencies, like their federal counterparts, participate in and review assessments of environmental impacts, in accordance with their responsibilities under federal or state laws.

  - A state historic preservation office advises and consults with federal and other state agencies to identify historic properties and assess and resolve adverse effects to them under the National Historic Preservation Act.

- *Local governments.* Local governments involved in highway projects include MPOs and rural planning organizations.

  - Every urbanized area with a population of 50,000 or more has an MPO, an organization made up of representatives of local governments—county, city, and town government officials—for the purpose of transportation planning and coordination of highway and transit projects. According to a nonprofit organization that represents MPOs, there are almost 400 MPOs in the United States.

  - Rural planning organizations are typically voluntary planning organizations that serve as a forum for local officials to develop consensus on regional transportation priorities for an area with a population of less than 50,000.

- *NGOs.* NGOs advocate for a number of issues, including the environment and transportation. Examples of NGOs include the following:

  - The Natural Resources Defense Council is an environmental organization that seeks to protect the environment by educating the public, lobbying government officials, and litigating, if necessary.

  - AASHTO advocates for transportation-related policies and provides technical transportation-related support to states.

- *Contractors.* Contractors generally are private sector companies that bid on contracts from federal and state transportation agencies to conduct various activities, such as conducting environmental studies or constructing a highway.

- *Private citizens.* Private citizens have the opportunity to provide comments and opinions in venues like public hearings.

Large Number of Steps in the Process

In addition to the involvement of a large number of stakeholders, completing a major highway project takes a number of years because of the many tasks, requirements, and approvals involved throughout the four phases of a highway project. Major highway projects can involve as many as 200 steps from the initial planning phase through the construction phase that require actions, approvals, or input from a number of stakeholders.[3]

Planning Phase

State DOTs and local planning organizations assess a project's purpose and consider the need for the project in relation to the need for other potential highway projects. To receive federal transportation funding, any project in an urbanized area must emerge from the relevant MPO and state DOT planning processes. For nonmetropolitan areas not covered by an MPO, states must consult with and provide opportunities for local officials to participate in statewide planning. To meet federal planning requirements, states must develop

---

[3]As previously noted, FHWA estimates that based on its 2009 data approximately 1 percent of all federal-aid highway projects in the United States were processed with an EIS. The vast majority of highway projects—96 percent—were processed as CEs under NEPA and generally did not require as many tasks to complete.

(1) a long-range statewide transportation plan covering a 20-year period and (2) a state transportation improvement program—that is, the state program of transportation projects covering at least a 4-year period that are to be supported with federal surface transportation funds, as well as regionally significant projects requiring an action by FHWA, whether or not federally funded.

Preliminary Design and Environmental Review Phase

During preliminary design, a project's location and design are identified, along with the effect, if any, of the proposed project and of potential alternatives on the environment; eventually, a preferred alternative is selected. Among other tasks, state DOTs identify the preliminary engineering issues, proposed alignment of roadways, and costs, as well as create topographic surveys and conduct traffic studies. During environmental review, the proposed project alternatives are examined and may require review, input, or feedback from relevant resource agencies such as USACE, FWS, or the Environmental Protection Agency. Environmental reviews require state and FHWA officials to address and comply with many federal laws—FHWA has identified over 40 environmental laws—as well as applicable state laws. More complex projects require additional time for the completion of preliminary designs and environmental reviews. In addition, private citizens and local governments are asked to comment on the project and its potential effects. At the end of this phase, the preferred alternative is selected.

Final Design and Right-of-Way Acquisition Phase

State DOTs finalize design plans, acquire property, and relocate utilities in the final design and right-of-way acquisition phase. State DOTs develop detailed engineering plans consistent with environmental documents and updated environmental studies, and finalize cost estimates. If a significant amount of time has passed since the preliminary design work was performed, right-of-way maps and other information may need to be updated. Acquiring property for the project includes determining any restrictions to state ownership of the property, determining the identities of property owners, making offers to property owners based on just compensation, negotiating a purchase price, relocating property owners and tenants, and sometimes invoking eminent domain. Utilities must be located, marked, surveyed, and possibly relocated. If there are a significant number of underground utilities, professional engineers, geologists, and land surveyors may be needed to determine the exact location of the utilities.

Construction Phase

State DOTs award construction contracts, oversee construction, and accept the completed project. State DOTs request and evaluate bids on projects and then award the contract. The federal government is not directly involved in construction, but does have an oversight role. For example, projects that receive federal-aid highway funds require FHWA concurrence on the award. During construction, the contractor and the state resolve any unexpected problems that may arise, such as removal of hazardous waste at the construction site. Once satisfied that construction has been carried out as agreed to with the contractor, the state must approve the final completion of construction.

Additional Factors That Can Affect Time Frames

In addition to the many stakeholders and tasks involved, a number of other factors can complicate the process and lead to longer highway project time frames such as the following:

Funding Availability

The availability of funding for large highway projects can affect how long it takes to complete a project. For example, one state DOT informed us it has completed a number of EISs for highway projects, but that these projects are stalled due to a lack of funds. In addition, a state DOT official stated that since the state did not have enough funding to complete major highway projects, they are choosing to focus more on completing smaller, less expensive highway projects such as bridge replacements and repaving. Of those responding to our survey, most state DOTs identified funding as a challenge for all project phases but found it to be more of a challenge in both the planning phase and the preliminary design and environmental review phase.[4]

Changing Transportation Priorities

Changes in a state's transportation priorities during a project's duration can complicate time frames and delay the project. For example, one administration may favor a highway project when it is first planned and may provide the necessary financial support; however, a new administration with different priorities may come in before the project is completed and withdraw or reduce support and funding. If a project that was shelved garners support again, in some cases, FHWA, the state DOT, or resource agencies might have to reevaluate, rework, and update environmental- or NEPA-related documents and information to ensure

---

[4]Specifically, 27 of 51 states (53 percent) identified funding as a "very great" or "substantial" challenge during the planning phase; 27 of 52 states (52 percent) identified funding as a "very great" or "substantial" challenge during the preliminary design and environmental review phase; 20 of 51 states (39 percent) identified funding as a "very great" or "substantial" challenge during the final design and right-of-way acquisition phase; and 17 of 50 states (34 percent) identified funding as a "very great" or "substantial" challenge during the construction phase.

GAO-12-593 Highway Projects

that the environmental impact information is current. This can lead to a longer project time frame.

Project Opposition

Public opposition and litigation can also lengthen highway project time frames or even lead to the cancellation of a project. For example, the Elizabeth Brady Road project in Orange County, North Carolina was canceled by FHWA due to public and local government opposition to the project. After the project began the preliminary design and environmental review phase, local community and government officials determined that there was insufficient need for the project because the potential costs outweighed the project's potential benefits. As a result, local government officials withdrew their support for the project and it was canceled. Public controversy related to a highway project can sometimes lead to litigation, which can also lengthen highway project time frames. Litigants might settle their lawsuit if, for example, a state DOT agrees to change the design of a project to limit its impact on a species or increase noise abatement measures. Lawsuits can also lead to longer completion time frames. For example, plaintiffs filed suit in 2006 against FHWA and the U.S. Forest Service for a highway project in Alaska, alleging that these parties failed to comply with a number of federal laws, including NEPA. The U.S. District Court found that the final EIS issued for the project was not valid and issued an injunction stopping all work on the project. Upon appeal, the U.S. Court of Appeals for the Ninth Circuit upheld the District Court decision.[5] In September 2011, nearly 5 years after the lawsuit was filed, the Alaska Department of Transportation and Public Facilities began work to prepare a supplemental EIS—that is, an updated EIS—for the project. The agency anticipates issuing a record of decision for this project in late 2013.

---

[5]Se. Alaska Conservation Council v. Fed. Highway Admin., 649 F.3d 1050 (9th Cir. 2011).

GAO-12-593 Highway Projects

State DOTs Generally Agree That SAFETEA-LU Provisions Could Decrease Project Time Frames but Find Some Provisions More Useful Than Others

States identified both benefits and challenges with each of the SAFETEA-LU provisions meant to help expedite highway projects but acknowledged alternative solutions for some of the provisions that better served their purposes. In our survey, state DOTs most frequently agreed that the Minor Impacts to Protected Public Land provision of SAFETEA-LU has the potential to save time (see table 2) and has relatively few challenges to implementation.[6]

---

[6]In our survey, we asked states to report the extent to which their agency agreed or disagreed that benefits, including time savings, could be realized from each of the SAFETEA-LU provisions we studied. For reporting purposes, we have combined responses of "strongly agree" and "agree," as well as "strongly disagree" and "disagree." Not all states responded to all questions asked in the survey.

Table 2: Potential Time Savings and Other Key Findings States Reported Regarding SAFETEA-LU Provisions Meant to Help Expedite Highway Projects, Since 2005

SAFETEA-LU provision	State agreement on potential time savings	Key findings states reported in GAO survey
Minor Impacts to Protected Public Land	92% (47 of 51 states)	States generally did not identify potential challenges with this provision. 82% of states disagreed that participation requirements for this provision are too challenging to fulfill, and nearly all states responding (47 of 49) have used this provision at least once.
Design-Build Contracting	79% (30 of 38 states)	Smaller highway projects, which comprise the majority of all highway projects, generally do not lend themselves to design-build contracting. Additionally, some states are prohibited by state statute from using this contracting method.
180-Day Statute of Limitations	78% (32 of 41 states)	Some states expressed concern that a shorter statute of limitations could draw undue attention to the project and encourage litigation.
Offering Financial Assistance to Stakeholder Agencies	77% (34 of 44 states)	Some states indicated that use of this provision has created a better working relationship between highway stakeholders; others noted that they saw limited results and have since stopped providing funding.
Categorical Exclusion Approval Authority	76% (34 of 45 states)	Almost two-thirds of states (29 out of 49) agreed that programmatic agreements could serve their agency better than this initiative. Only three states—Alaska, California, and Utah—participate in this program.
Issue Resolution Process	61% (22 of 36 states)	No state has used this provision, choosing instead to resolve issues at the lowest possible staff level or to follow procedures established in programmatic agreements.
NEPA Approval Authority	56% (19 of 34 states)	States expressed reluctance to accept federal court jurisdiction in order to participate in this pilot program, an action they generally refer to as 'waiving their sovereign immunity.' Only one state—California—is participating in this pilot program.

Source: GAO.

Minor Impacts to Protected Public Land

Most respondents agreed that the Minor Impacts to Protected Public Land provision of SAFETEA-LU has potential time savings benefits, and nearly all have used this provision at least once. This provision authorizes an historic site or publicly owned land from a park, recreation area, or wildlife or waterfowl refuge, to be used for a transportation program or project if a DOT determines that such use would result in minor impacts (i.e., "de minimis impacts") to that resource.[7] The Department of Transportation Act of 1966 includes a provision—known as Section 4(f)—which stipulates that FHWA and other DOT agencies cannot approve the use of

---

[7]With respect to historic sites, a DOT may make a finding of de minimis impact if, among other things, it receives written concurrence from the applicable state historic preservation officer or tribal historic preservation officer. With respect to parks, recreation areas, or wildlife or waterfowl refuges, the DOT may make a finding of de minimis impact if, among other things, it receives written concurrence from the officials with jurisdiction over the park, recreation area, or wildlife or waterfowl refuge.

land from publicly owned parks, recreational areas, wildlife and waterfowl refuges, or public and private historical sites unless (1) there is no feasible and prudent alternative to the use of such land and (2) the action includes all possible planning to minimize harm to the property resulting from use.[8] Complying with Section 4(f) can result in additional time to receive project approval. One NGO we spoke with noted that use of the Minor Impacts to Protected Public Land provision of SAFETEA-LU is a more "common sense" approach that not only allows greater use of these protected properties when only very minor impacts are likely to occur, but also helps to expedite highway projects.

- *Potential benefits.* Of those responding to our survey, 92 percent of states (47 of 51 states) agreed that this SAFETEA-LU provision has the potential to save time. In addition, of those responding, 80 percent (41 of 51 states) identified the Minor Impacts to Protected Public Land provision as having the potential to create staffing or personnel savings and 59 percent (29 of 49 states) identified the provision as having the potential to increase the number of projects completed.

- *Potential challenges.* Most states who responded to our survey did not indicate significant challenges to implementing this SAFETEA-LU provision. For example, 82 percent of states (42 of 51 states) disagreed that the participation requirements for this provision are too challenging to fulfill, indicating that this provision may be easier to use or implement than the other provisions.

- *Implementation/use.* Of all the SAFETEA-LU provisions we studied, the Minor Impacts to Protected Public Land provision was used most frequently. Of those states responding, almost all (47 of 49 states) had used this provision at least once, with 9 states indicating that they have used this provision for more than 50 percent of their highway projects since SAFETEA-LU's enactment in 2005.

Design-Build Contracting

Most states responding to our survey agreed that the Design-Build Contracting provision within SAFETEA-LU has the potential to save time, but many states have not used this contracting method and, therefore, have not had the opportunity to take advantage of this provision. Under the traditional procurement approach, design and construction services must be separated and a construction contract, which generally goes to

---

[8]23 U.S.C. § 138(a) and (b).

the lowest bidder, can be awarded only after the design is complete. Design-build contracting combines the responsibilities for designing and constructing a project in a single contract instead of separating these responsibilities. The Design-Build Contracting provision in SAFETEA-LU repealed the minimum cost requirements for use of design-build contracting for federal-aid highway projects; prior to enactment of SAFETEA-LU, federal-aid highway projects needed to have total costs exceed $50 million in order to use design-build contracting.

In our survey, state DOTs generally agreed that the Design-Build Contracting provision has the potential to save time, but noted some challenges and limited use.

- *Potential benefits.* Of those responding, 79 percent of states (30 of 38 states) agreed that this SAFETEA-LU provision has the potential to save time. Fewer states that responded agreed that other benefits could potentially be realized from use of design-build contracting: 45 percent (17 of 38 states) noted that its use could potentially increase the number of highway projects completed, and 37 percent (14 of 38 states) noted potential staff or personnel savings.

- *Potential challenges.* Most states did not indicate significant challenges to using this SAFETEA-LU provision in the survey questions we asked.[9] However, states did provide some challenges to design-build contracting in their written responses. For example, some states are prohibited by state statute from using design-build contracting for highway projects. Other states noted that problems in completing other project tasks, such as obtaining permits, can slow overall project completion time frames such that potential time savings achieved by design-build contracting might be negated.

- *Implementation/use.* Of those responding, 60 percent of states (26 of 43 states) have used design-build contracting at least once since enactment of SAFETEA-LU. However, the majority of states that responded (24 of 43 states, or 56 percent) use design-build

---

[9]We asked states the extent to which they agreed or disagreed that the following two issues are challenges that could be faced: (1) programmatic agreements could serve their agency better than this initiative and (2) state or agency policy discourages the use of this initiative. Only 4 out of 37 states agreed or strongly agreed that the first issue could be a challenge, and 8 out of 34 agreed or strongly agreed that the second could be a challenge.

contracting for less than 10 percent of all highway projects. States noted both in our survey and in our interviews that smaller highway projects—such as resurfacing or landscaping projects that are processed as CEs—generally do not require extensive design work and, as a result, do not lend themselves to the use of design-build contracting.

180-Day Statute of Limitations

Most states responding to our survey agreed that the 180-Day Statute of Limitations provision has potential benefits, and many have had at least one highway project since SAFETEA-LU's enactment that has taken advantage of it. Prior to enactment of SAFETEA-LU, individuals or organizations generally had up to 6 years in which they could file a judicial claim on a final agency action related to environmental requirements, such as NEPA requirements. This provision of SAFETEA-LU bars claims seeking judicial review of a permit, license, or approval issued by a federal agency for a highway project unless that claim is filed within 180 days of a notice in the *Federal Register*—FHWA generally publishes these notices—announcing the final agency action.

In our survey, state DOTs generally agreed that the 180-Day Statute of Limitations provision has the potential to save time, and many states have taken advantage of this provision since SAFETEA-LU's enactment; however, some states expressed concerns that a shorter statute of limitations could actually encourage litigation.

- *Potential benefits*. Of those responding, 78 percent (32 of 41 states) agreed that this SAFETEA-LU provision has the potential to save time. 56 percent of those states responding (22 of 39 states) also agreed that this provision could result in staff or personnel savings. Only about one-third of those responding (15 of 41 states, or 37 percent) agreed that the provision could result in more projects being completed.

- *Potential challenges*. When asked what challenges, if any, could be faced from this SAFETEA-LU provision, 8 states noted that a shorter statute of limitations may actually encourage litigation.[10] In general, these 8 states noted that if the shorter statute of limitations was used, such use could be seen as suspect by outside entities and encourage them to question the project and file a lawsuit against it.

- *Implementation/use.* Due in part to the above mentioned challenge, at least one state has chosen not to take advantage of the shorter statute of limitations. Of those states responding to our survey, 64 percent (29 of 45 states) have used the 180-Day Statute of Limitations provision for at least one project since enactment of SAFETEA-LU, leaving 36 percent of states (16 of 45 states) as having never used the provision. Officials from one state DOT we interviewed did note that they have chosen to not pursue this shorter statute of limitations as they feel its use might draw undue attention to the project and encourage outside entities to litigate it.

Offering Financial Assistance to Stakeholder Agencies

Most states responding to our survey agreed that the Offering Financial Assistance to Stakeholder Agencies provision of SAFETEA-LU has potential benefits, including time and staffing or personnel savings, but fewer states have actually taken advantage of this provision. Under this SAFETEA-LU provision, a state DOT can use part of its federal highway funding to support staff for a federal or state agency participating in the environmental review process, such as the local USACE or FWS office. Funds provided in accordance with this provision may only be used for projects in a given state that support activities that directly and meaningfully contribute to expediting and improving transportation project planning and completion.

In our survey, state DOTs generally agreed that the Offering Financial Assistance to Stakeholder Agencies provision has the potential to save time, but its use is not as widespread as some of the other SAFETEA-LU provisions.

---

[10]We asked states to provide a written response to the following question: "What challenges, if any, could be faced from the statute of limitations provision established in SAFETEA-LU Section 6002?" Twenty-five states provided some form of a written response, with one state noting two challenges. Of those, 8 states provided a response indicating that a shorter statute of limitations could encourage others to file a lawsuit against a project; 10 provided a response indicating that they did not have a comment or that the provision was beneficial; and 8 states' responses indicated a unique challenge.

- *Potential benefits.* Of those responding, 77 percent of states (34 of 44 states) agreed that this SAFETEA-LU provision has the potential to save time. The majority of those states responding also agreed that this provision could have potential staff or personnel savings (26 of 44 states, or 59 percent), as well as increase the number of projects completed (25 of 44 states, or 57 percent).

- *Potential challenges.* States responding to our survey generally noted some challenges to using this SAFETEA-LU provision. Nineteen of 44 states (43 percent) responding agreed that programmatic agreements could serve their agency better than this SAFETEA-LU provision. However, only 9 percent of states (4 of 43 states) agreed that a state or agency policy would discourage them from providing financial assistance to affected entities.

- *Implementation/use.* Of those responding, 58 percent of states (25 of 43 states) have provided financial assistance to affected entities at least once. However, a large number (18 of 43 states, or 42 percent) have never taken advantage of this provision. In our interviews with state DOTs and federal resource agencies, interviewees also had mixed opinions on this SAFETEA-LU provision. For example, some interviewees stated that use of this SAFETEA-LU provision has created a better working relationship between the state DOT and the affected entity. However, other states we interviewed indicated that they had previously provided financial assistance to affected entities but had seen limited results and had stopped providing such funding. Staff from the federal resource agencies we spoke with were generally familiar with this SAFETEA-LU provision and, in some cases, found it to be helpful in expediting the completion of highway projects.

Categorical Exclusion Approval Authority

While most states responding to our survey agreed that the Categorical Exclusion Approval Authority provision within SAFETEA-LU has the potential to save time, only three states are participating in this program, and most states indicated that other techniques could achieve the same outcome as this program. This SAFETEA-LU provision authorizes U.S. DOT to assign and a state to assume responsibility for determining whether certain designated activities constitute actions that are categorically excluded from the requirement to prepare an EA or EIS. As noted above, most highway projects in the United States are processed as CEs, thus many of the projects a state DOT leads could be affected by participation in this program. As of April 2012, only three states are participating in this program: Alaska, California, and Utah. These three states have signed memoranda of agreement with their respective FHWA division offices outlining the processes and procedures they are to follow once assuming authority to approve CEs. Per SAFETEA-LU, these agreements are to last no more than 3 years, but can be renewed by mutual agreement of both the state DOT and FHWA. States that choose to participate in this program are required to accept federal court jurisdiction for the decisions they make under the program.[11] Highway stakeholders often refer to this aspect of the Categorical Exclusion Approval Authority provision as requiring the state legislature to 'waive its sovereign immunity.'

In our survey, state DOTs generally agreed that the Categorical Exclusion Approval Authority provision has the potential to save time, but several respondents supported the use of approaches other than this program to achieve a similar outcome.

- *Potential benefits.* Of those responding, 76 percent (34 of 45 states) agreed that this SAFETEA-LU provision has the potential to save time. States also saw this provision as having the potential to increase the number of projects being completed (26 of 44 states, or 59 percent) and create staffing or personnel savings (22 of 45 states, or 49 percent).

- *Potential challenges.* The majority of those responding to our survey (29 of 49 states, or 59 percent), as well as some state DOTs we spoke with, indicated that the use of agreements—such as programmatic agreements or memoranda of agreement—could serve the state DOTs better than this SAFETEA-LU provision. Seventeen state DOTs noted in our survey that they have undertaken efforts to establish agreements with their respective FHWA division offices or federal and state resource agencies. Among other things, these agreements establish policies and procedures for the state DOTs to follow in certain situations and scenarios. For example, the Missouri DOT has entered into a programmatic agreement with the FHWA division office to allow the state DOT to classify certain activities specified in the agreement as CEs without submitting each project to FHWA for approval of an environmental classification of CE.

---

[11]More specifically, 23 U.S.C. § 326(c)(3) states: "In a memorandum of understanding, the State shall consent to accept the jurisdiction of the Federal courts for the compliance, discharge, and enforcement of any responsibility of the Secretary [of Transportation] that the State assumes."

Agreements such as these allow relevant agencies—in this case, the FHWA division office—to make certain that projects comply with relevant laws and regulations but relieve the agency of the burden of having to review every project that the state DOT undertakes.

- *Implementation/use.* As noted above, only three states—Alaska, California, and Utah—are participating in the program created by this SAFETEA-LU provision. All three state DOTs indicated that they have seen positive outcomes from their participation in the program.

Issue Resolution Process

States saw the Issue Resolution Process provision within SAFETEA-LU as having some potential to save time, but none has used this provision, and most saw the use of written agreements between parties—including programmatic agreements or memoranda of understanding—as a better alternative. This SAFETEA-LU provision established procedures for resolving issues that could delay completion of the environmental review process or could result in denial of approvals required for the project under specific laws, such as the Clean Water Act or the Endangered Species Act. In general terms, a meeting of the relevant agencies can be convened to resolve the issues at hand; if a resolution cannot be achieved, the lead agency—for most federal-aid highway projects, this would be FHWA—is to notify a number of interested parties, including the Senate Committee on Environment and Public Works, the House Committee on Transportation and Infrastructure, and the Council on Environmental Quality within the Executive Office of the President.

In our survey, state DOTs indicated that this SAFETEA-LU provision has some potential to create time savings but generally saw the use of programmatic agreements as a better alternative for resolving issues between parties.

- *Potential benefits.* Of those responding, 61 percent (22 of 36 states) agreed that this SAFETEA-LU provision has the potential to save time. States generally did not agree that other potential benefits could arise from the use of this SAFETEA-LU provision: 37 percent (14 of 38 states) agreed that its use has the potential to create staffing or personnel savings, and only 29 percent (11 of 38 states) agreed that its use could increase the number of projects completed.

- *Potential challenges.* The majority of the states responding to this portion of the survey (25 of 41 states, or 61 percent) indicated that established agreements, like a programmatic agreement, could better serve their agency than this SAFETEA-LU provision. Some of the state DOTs we interviewed indicated that they had programmatic agreements in place with various parties, such as federal resource agencies, that established procedures by which issues could be identified and resolved. States and federal resource agencies told us that they would prefer if issues were identified and resolved at lower staff levels, rather than by management or executives, or through the process established in this SAFETEA-LU provision.

- *Implementation/use.* As noted above, this SAFETEA-LU provision has not been used or implemented, and highway stakeholders we interviewed noted that resolving these disputes using methods other than this SAFETEA-LU provision are preferred.

NEPA Approval Authority

The majority of states responding to our survey agreed that the NEPA Approval Authority provision within SAFETEA-LU has the potential to save time, but most states indicated that it is too burdensome to begin participating. This SAFETEA-LU provision required the establishment of a pilot program to permit not more than five states to assume certain federal environmental review responsibilities, such as the environmental reviews required under NEPA or other federal laws.[12] SAFETEA-LU listed five states that were given the opportunity to participate in this pilot program: Alaska, California, Ohio, Oklahoma, and Texas. To date, California is the only state that is participating in this pilot program. Other states expressed interest but withdrew their applications to participate. Eventually, FHWA opened the pilot program to all states, but limited participation to a total of five states, as called for in SAFETEA-LU. Much like the Categorical Exclusion Approval Authority provision of SAFETEA-LU, states that choose to participate in this program are required to accept federal court jurisdiction for the decisions they make under the program, an action which is generally undertaken by the state legislature and which highway stakeholders often referred to as requiring the state legislature to 'waive its sovereign immunity.'

In our survey, state DOTs agreed that the NEPA Approval Authority pilot program has the potential to save time, but a majority of respondents

---

[12]Pursuant to SAFETEA-LU, the DOT Secretary may not assign responsibility for any conformity determination required under section 176 of the Clean Air Act or any responsibility imposed on the Secretary related to transportation planning as established in 23 U.S.C. §§ 134, 135. See 23 U.S.C. § 327.

indicated that participation requirements for this provision are too challenging to fulfill.

- *Potential benefits.* Of those responding, 56 percent of states (19 of 34 states) agreed that this SAFETEA-LU provision has the potential to save time. States generally agreed that this provision does not have the potential to save staffing or personnel resources, or increase the number of projects completed.[13]

- *Potential challenges.* The majority of states responding to this section of our survey (27 of 33 states, or 82 percent) indicated that the participation requirements for this initiative are too challenging to fulfill. This message was reiterated in interviews we conducted with state DOTs. For example, officials from these agencies stated that accepting federal court jurisdiction for the environmental review decisions they make was something they, their agency management, or their state legislature—which would need to approve the acceptance of such responsibility—did not wish to take on.

- *Implementation/use.* As noted above, California is the only state that is currently participating in this pilot program. According to the California Department of Transportation, highway projects requiring an EA now take about 30 months less to complete than they previously did. In addition, staff from some of the federal resource agencies we spoke with indicated that California's participation in the pilot program has generally been beneficial, with staff from one resource agency calling for California's continued participation in the pilot program. While California has reported a time savings from its participation in the NEPA Approval Authority pilot program, other states with whom we spoke did not express interest in this pilot program, with most states citing the requirement to accept federal court jurisdiction for the decisions they make under the program as a key reason why they do not wish to participate. In addition, at least two states indicated that they appreciate having FHWA make these environmental decisions. More specifically, they stated that FHWA has the staff and expertise to make informed decisions regarding environmental impacts.

---

[13]Of the states responding, 6 out of 35 agreed that staffing or personnel savings could be realized, and 7 out of 35 agreed that an increased number of projects could be completed from using this provision.

States and FHWA Have Initiated Efforts to Develop and Share Innovative Practices for Expediting Highway Projects

States have implemented a variety of efforts to expedite highway projects, and FHWA has initiated efforts to share innovative practices. Some state efforts began in the 1990s in response to challenges faced at that time. Other state efforts are more recent, prompted by new authorities provided by SAFETEA-LU or by streamlining concepts recently promoted by FHWA. FHWA is making efforts to share innovative practices to help expedite highway projects, most recently through an effort known as Every Day Counts. However, it is too soon to determine the effect these initiatives have had on highway project time frames.

States Have Implemented Streamlining Practices Spanning All Project Phases

Most states have made efforts to expedite projects with state DOTs playing a key role in choosing the techniques that are used. In our survey of state DOTs, we asked officials about initiatives they have undertaken since the enactment of SAFETEA-LU to expedite the four phases of highway projects. Most states—43—reported that they have implemented at least 1 initiative, 4 states reported undertaking no initiatives, 3 states did not respond for any phase, and 2 states reported no initiatives for some phases and no response for other phases. According to the survey, states most often implemented initiatives involving the preliminary design and environmental review phase (39 states). Twenty-two states reported implementing initiatives involving the planning phase, 15 states involving the final design and right-of-way acquisition phase, and 19 states involving the construction phase. We also asked officials about the potential benefits that could be realized from the initiatives they had undertaken. For each of the four phases of a highway project, time savings was the benefit most often cited by states.[14] Staff savings was cited as a potential benefit by a majority of states for all phases except construction, when it was cited as a potential benefit by 39 percent of the states (7 of 18 states) responding. Increased number of projects completed was cited as a benefit by a majority of officials responding for all phases except construction, where it was cited as a potential benefit by half of the states responding (9 of 18).

---

[14]For each of the four phases of highway projects, we asked states the extent to which they agreed or disagreed that time savings, staffing/personnel savings, and increased number of projects completed are potential benefits of initiatives they have undertaken. The numbers of states that agreed or strongly agreed that time savings are a potential benefit are: planning phase—18 out of 21 states; preliminary design and environmental review phase—36 out of 39 states; final design and right-of-way acquisition phase—15 out of 15 states; and construction phase—18 out of 18 states.

State DOTs reported implementing a variety of types of initiatives to expedite highway projects but generally not one type more than another. In fact, only 4 of more than 30 initiatives were reported by 10 or more states:

- *Linking Planning and Environmental Review.* Twenty-three states reported implementing steps that linked their planning and environmental review processes. Using information collected in the planning phase and carrying it through the environmental review phase can minimize duplication of effort and reduce delays in project implementation. For example, the North Carolina Department of Transportation designed a project development process, implemented in 1997, that promotes early involvement of state and federal stakeholders. Each project must pass seven concurrence points that cover aspects of project planning, environmental review, and permitting. This process reduces permit processing times from years to months, according to North Carolina Department of Transportation officials.

- *Using Programmatic Agreements.* Seventeen states reported implementing programmatic agreements. These written documents establish a process for consultation, review, and compliance with one or more federal laws between one or more parties, such as a state DOT and a resource agency. Programmatic agreements can help reduce project time frames. For example, an agreement between the Illinois Department of Transportation and FHWA created both a procedure for negotiating project-specific time frames for completing environmental reviews and completion time goals for EISs and EAs. After processing five EISs and four EAs under the agreement, project completion time was reduced by at least 2 years, according to a 2010 AASHTO report for FHWA. Some state DOTs have used programmatic agreements for more than a decade, including at least four states that have used programmatic agreements since the 1990s. An agreement between the California Department of Transportation, FHWA, and four resource agencies has been in place since 1991.

- *Using Design-Build Contracts.* Eleven states reported implementing design-build contracts. Again, design-build contracting combines the responsibilities for designing and constructing a project in a single contract instead of separating these responsibilities. Design-build contracting can provide significant time savings compared with the design-bid-build approach where design and construction phases must take place in sequence, according to FHWA.

- *Using Other Nontraditional Construction Contracts.* Eleven states reported implementing other nontraditional construction contracts. These included construction manager/general contractor contracts[15] and other nontraditional contract approaches such as cost plus time bidding, lane rentals, and contractor completion incentives and disincentives.[16]

State DOTs also reported implementing several other highway project streamlining initiatives, including use of electronic bidding, clarifying the scope of preliminary design, linking the final design and right-of-way acquisition phase with prior project development phases, as well as early right-of-way purchases.

FHWA Is Sharing Practices Among States Though It Is Too Soon to Know the Outcome

FHWA is sharing information on methods to expedite highway projects with state DOTs through an effort called Every Day Counts. This effort's goals are to shorten project time frames and accelerate use of technology and innovation by convincing states to adopt proven, rapidly deployable innovations. Many of these innovations were in use by some states before they were selected for promotion through Every Day Counts: as discussed earlier, for example, California's 1991 programmatic agreement or North Carolina's 1997 project development process. FHWA selected its Every Day Counts innovations through a process that involved headquarters and division office staff, as well as outside organizations such as AASHTO, Associated General Contractors, and the American Road and Transportation Builders Association. Every Day Counts was introduced at AASHTO meetings in spring 2010 and subsequently promoted at 10 regional summits sponsored by FHWA and

---

[15]The construction manager/general contractor method allows a state to hire a contractor early in the design process in order to benefit from the contractor's constructability input as the design develops. The method can save time, compared with the traditional method, because construction can start before designs are complete. Under the traditional method, design and construction phases must take place in sequence.

[16]*Cost plus time bidding* is a contracting procedure that selects the low bidder based on a monetary combination of the contract bid items and the time needed to complete the project. *Lane rental* is a contracting technique by which a contractor is charged a fee for occupying existing highway lanes or shoulders during construction. The fee motivates the contractor to minimize the time that a lane or a shoulder is out of service, minimizing traffic delay to highway users. *Contractor completion incentives and disincentives* are contract provisions that pay the contractor a certain amount of money for each day a highway project is completed ahead of schedule and charge money for each day the contractor overruns scheduled time.

AASHTO. Each state was asked to decide on specific initiatives it wanted to pursue and develop a plan for implementing them during 2011 and 2012. States were also asked to create transportation innovation councils to track attainment of goals. Under Every Day Counts, FHWA urged state DOTs to consider use of 15 specific initiatives—10 designed to shorten project time frames and 5 designed to accelerate technology deployment. The Every Day Counts initiatives described below include 3 of the 4 initiatives that states have taken as described above. See table 3 for brief descriptions of the initiatives in FHWA's Every Day Counts effort for implementation in 2011 and 2012 and appendix II for more detailed information on those Every Day Counts initiatives. FHWA expects to introduce a new set of initiatives in late 2012, to be implemented during 2013 and 2014, and intends that another series of initiatives will follow for the period from 2015 to 2016. FHWA began, in October 2011, the process of soliciting ideas for new initiatives to implement in 2013, saying it would consider proposed initiatives based on factors such as transportation system impact, readiness for deployment, affordability, and urgency.

Table 3: FHWA's Every Day Counts Initiatives for 2011 and 2012

Title	Description
Initiatives to shorten project time frames	
Linking planning and environmental review	Promotes use of planning documents and decisions from the project planning process in the environmental review process. This can minimize duplication of effort and reduce delays in project implementation.
Early consultation with FHWA environmental attorneys	Consulting with FHWA environmental attorneys at early decision points can help decision makers avoid problems later, saving time and costs.
Expanded use of programmatic agreements	A programmatic agreement formally spells out the terms of an agreement between a state DOT and other state and/or federal agencies.
Compensatory mitigation	Various laws require compensatory mitigation for projects that cause unavoidable impacts to streams, wetlands, and other waters. Compensatory mitigation can be accomplished through mitigation banks or in-lieu fee programs.[a]
Clarifying scope of preliminary design	States can complete design activities not required for a NEPA determination under preliminary design. When performed concurrently with the NEPA process, these activities can expedite highway projects without affecting eligibility for federal aid.
Allowable right-of-way acquisition streamlining	To save time, states can acquire property using techniques such as appraisal waiver valuations, incentive payments to advance acquisition and relocation, and appraisals and negotiations of property acquisition (up to $10,000) by the same individual.
Effective coordination for utility relocation	States can effectively coordinate utility relocation during project development by techniques such as documenting the terms and considerations for accomplishing utility relocation, and financing the work in an effective and timely manner.
FHWA technical assistance for stalled projects	FHWA subject matter experts, drawn from offices nationwide, provide assistance to highway stakeholders to help resolve issues that would otherwise hold up the NEPA review. These staff can help resolve resource-specific issues concerning wetlands, endangered species, and cultural resources.
Use of design-build contracts	Design-build contracts combine design and construction tasks into one contract, eliminating the separate bid phase and allowing certain aspects of design and construction to take place at the same time.
Use of construction manager/general contractor contracts	The owners of a project hire either a general contractor or design firm to serve as the construction manager, placing responsibility for design review, design modifications, system integration, and construction with that single contractor.
Initiatives to accelerate technology deployment	
Warm mix asphalt paving	Asphalt is produced and placed on the road at lower temperatures than the conventional hot-mix method. By extending the construction season, warm mix asphalt allows projects to be completed faster.
Prefabricated bridge elements	An old bridge can be demolished while the new bridge elements are built at the same time off-site, then brought to the project location ready to erect.
Integrated bridge support technology	Use of alternating layers of fill material and fabric reinforcement sheets to provide support for small bridges and reduce construction time.
Pavement Safety Edge	Saves lives by allowing drivers who stray off highways to return to the road safely. Instead of a vertical drop-off, the Safety Edge shapes the edge of the pavement to an angle that allows drivers to reenter the roadway safely.
Adaptive signal control technology	This technology adjusts the timing of red, yellow, and green lights to accommodate changing traffic patterns and ease traffic congestion.

Source: FHWA.

[a]A mitigation bank is a large-scale mitigation site approved through the federal Clean Water Act and other state programs for resource protection. In mitigation banking, infrastructure developers buy credits from the bank sponsor before any impacts occur. An in-lieu fee program conducts wetland, stream, or threatened or endangered species habitat restoration, creation, enhancement, or preservation. In-lieu fee programs must be administered by government entities or nonprofits. Users of the program pay the program sponsor for mitigation credits. See more detailed explanations of these programs in appendix II.

FHWA has developed performance measures for Every Day Counts that are linked to U.S. DOT performance measures, but it is too soon to determine the effect these initiatives have had on expediting highway projects, according to an FHWA official. FHWA and other highway project stakeholders developed one or two performance measures for each of the Every Day Counts initiatives. For example, FHWA established the following performance measure for the "Expanding Use of Programmatic Agreements" under Every Day Counts: "FHWA will expand, revise, or create 15 programmatic agreements at the state and regional scale by December 30, 2011." These performance measures support the overall goals of the Every Day Counts effort, which the FHWA administrator has stated are "to cut project delivery time in half and more quickly advance innovation into daily practice." The Every Day Counts performance measures and goals that FHWA established are linked to a U.S. DOT performance measure, an attribute of successful performance measures.[17] Specifically, since fiscal year 2010, U.S. DOT has had a performance measure to streamline environmental review with a target of 48 months to complete an EIS for major transportation projects.[18] U.S. DOT noted in its fiscal year 2011 performance report that Every Day Counts is an effort to help reduce project times. Every Day Counts includes 13 specific initiatives to streamline time frames for all four phases of highway projects, including the environmental review phase. While FHWA has collected data to address the U.S. DOT target noted above and data on the Every Day Counts initiatives, states have only had about 1 year to implement the Every Day Counts initiatives and, according to an FHWA official, it is too soon to tell if those initiatives have had a positive effect on expediting the completion of highway projects.

---

[17]Past GAO work has identified nine attributes of successful performance measures, including linkage, meaning that performance goals and measures at the operational level should align with an agency's goals and mission. See GAO, *Tax Administration: IRS Needs to Further Refine Its Tax Filing Season Performance Measures,* GAO-03-143 (Washington. D.C: Nov. 22, 2002).

[18]The time to complete an EIS is generally measured from the date the notice of intent is issued to the date the record of decision is issued.

For fiscal year 2011, FHWA reported that the median time to complete EISs was 79 months (about 6.6 years). However, FHWA also reported that 16 of the EISs completed during fiscal year 2011 were started before August 2005, when SAFETEA-LU was enacted, and the median time to complete those EISs was 110 months (about 9 years). For the 7 remaining EISs completed during 2011, the median time to completion was 44 months (a little under 3.7 years). These data suggest that the full impact of the Every Day Counts initiatives on the time to complete EISs may not be discernable for several years, if ever, due to a number of reasons. Such reasons could include (1) the lengthy time frames needed to adopt complex initiatives such as linking planning and environmental review or compensatory mitigation,[19] (2) the possibility of EISs being completed which had started before SAFETEA-LU was enacted or Every Day Counts began, or (3) the impact of the SAFETEA-LU provisions discussed above that were also meant to expedite highway projects.

FHWA's efforts to share promising practices depend on the willingness of state DOTs to adopt them. Each state has identified Every Day Counts initiatives to use, according to an FHWA report. An FHWA headquarters official provided the following examples of Every Day Counts initiatives that have achieved wide acceptance:

- States have, since the introduction of Every Day Counts, generated 56 new programmatic agreements, far more than the Every Day Counts goal of 15 programmatic agreements by December 2011.

- Nearly all states are using warm mix asphalt. Interest in the product increased after FHWA promoted it as an Every Day Counts initiative.

- Over 40 states are using prefabricated bridge elements. They report working on 663 bridges, far more than the Every Day Counts goal of designing or building 100 bridges by December 2012.

---

[19]One state, cited by FHWA as a case study at linking planning and environmental review, took 21 months getting from the summit meeting that introduced the new integrated planning system concept to the memorandum of understanding signed by 24 agencies that agreed to support the new system. Another state, cited by FHWA as a case study at implementing compensatory mitigation, spent 18 months developing its memorandum of agreement to implement the mitigation concept developed at a workshop.

Concluding Observations

Completing major highway projects involves a complex process that depends on a wide range of stakeholders conducting many tasks. The long time frames to complete highway projects are often caused by factors outside the control of state DOTs, such as a lack of available funds, changes in a state's transportation priorities, or litigation. These factors can be project specific and may not be controllable by legislation, or by federal or state initiatives.

The SAFETEA-LU provisions meant to help expedite highway projects are generally viewed by state DOTs as having the potential to save time. However, given that state DOTs noted in our survey that there are other solutions outside of the SAFETEA-LU provisions that better serve their needs and are within their authority to implement, it is unlikely that state DOTs will greatly increase their participation in some of the SAFETEA-LU provisions we analyzed, particularly those that delegate environmental review decision-making authority from FHWA to state DOTs and require the state to accept federal court jurisdiction for such decisions. Regardless, keeping these provisions in law would continue to give state DOTs the ability to pursue these provisions should they later choose to do so.

FHWA's Every Day Counts effort offers a structured approach to collecting and sharing information with state DOTs to help expedite highway projects. FHWA's continued efforts to (1) track the progress of Every Day Counts using the performance measures it developed for each initiative and (2) use Every Day Counts as a way to keep introducing new initiatives for trial and adoption by state DOTs can help to ensure that promising practices are developed and shared among states. Additionally, use of the Every Day Counts effort could help U.S. DOT as it attempts to meet its performance measure to streamline environmental review.

Agency Comments

We provided U.S. DOT with a draft of this report for review and comment. U.S. DOT provided technical comments, which we incorporated as appropriate.

As agreed with your offices, unless you publicly announce the contents of this report earlier, we plan no further distribution until 30 days from the report date. At that time, we will send copies to the appropriate congressional committees; the Secretary of Transportation; the Administrator, Federal Highway Administration; and other interested parties. In addition, the report will be available at no charge on the GAO website at http://www.gao.gov.

If you or your staff members have any questions about this report, please contact me at (202) 512-2834 or wised@gao.gov. Contact points for our Offices of Congressional Relations and Public Affairs may be found on the last page of this report. GAO staff who made key contributions to this report are listed in appendix III.

David J. Wise
Director, Physical Infrastructure Issues

Appendix I: Objectives, Scope and Methodology

Our work for this report was focused on federal-aid highway projects and efforts to expedite those projects. In particular, this report addresses the following questions: (1) What is the process for planning, designing, and constructing federally funded highway projects, and what factors could affect project time frames? (2) What are state departments of transportation (DOT) views on the benefits and challenges of implementing initiatives to expedite highway projects established by the Safe, Accountable, Flexible, Efficient Transportation Equity Act: A Legacy for Users (SAFETEA-LU)? (3) What practices have state DOTs and the Federal Highway Administration (FHWA) implemented to expedite highway projects?

To describe the process for completing highway projects, as well as the factors that could affect project time frames, we reviewed and analyzed relevant legislation—particularly SAFETEA-LU—regulations, congressional hearing statements, and relevant reports and other publications. We also conducted a number of interviews in six states to collect information on practices involved in completing highway projects, as well as factors that could affect project time frames (see table 4). We chose these six states using several criteria, including participation in the environmental review delegation programs established under SAFETEA-LU (i.e., the Categorical Exclusion Approval Authority and the NEPA Approval Authority provisions), number of active and inactive environmental impact statements, amount of federal highway funding received in fiscal year 2011, and geographic location within the United States. The six states we chose to interview were Alaska, California, Missouri, North Carolina, Pennsylvania, and Utah. In each state, we interviewed the FHWA division office and the state DOT. To obtain more detailed information on processes to complete highway projects—but to minimize the burden on interviewees and in the interest of time—we interviewed regional offices of key resource agencies in two of the six states we selected: California and North Carolina.[1] We chose these states based on geographic diversity, as well as previously conducted fieldwork. We selected six resource agencies to interview, as they were often cited in our preliminary review of reports, publications, and other documents, as well as in early interviews with state DOTs. The resource agencies we interviewed were: U.S. Army Corps of Engineers, U.S.

---

[1] In general, the Advisory Council on Historic Preservation—the federal resource agency responsible for historic preservation—delegates much of its authority under the National Historic Preservation Act to state historic preservation offices.

Environmental Protection Agency, U.S. Fish and Wildlife Service, U.S.
Forest Service, National Marine Fisheries Service, and state historic
preservation offices. There are potentially other federal—as well as state,
local, and tribal—agencies that could have been interviewed, but we
chose to limit our scope to these six federal agencies. These interviews
are not generalizable to all states. Furthermore, for this report, we
focused only on federal-aid highways and not other types of highways.

Table 4: Highway Project Stakeholders Interviewed

Agency	Headquarters office	Alaska	California	Missouri	North Carolina	Pennsylvania	Utah
FHWA	✓	✓	✓	✓	✓	✓	✓
State DOT		✓	✓	✓	✓	✓	✓
Advisory Council on Historic Preservation/State Historic Preservation Office	✓		✓		✓		
U.S. Army Corps of Engineers	✓		✓		✓		
U.S. Environmental Protection Agency	✓		✓		✓		
U.S. Fish and Wildlife Service	✓		✓		✓		
U.S. Forest Service	✓		✓		✓		
National Marine Fisheries Service	✓		✓		✓		

Source: GAO.

To identify state DOT perspectives on the benefits and challenges
associated with implementing provisions meant to help expedite highway
projects established in SAFETEA-LU, we (1) reviewed information
obtained in the above mentioned interviews and (2) conducted a survey
of state DOTs. To conduct this survey, we identified key provisions within
SAFETEA-LU that we felt were meant to expedite highway projects based
on our review of the legislation, analysis of relevant reports, and
interviews with highway project stakeholders. We then developed a draft
survey to gather state DOTs' perspectives on the benefits and challenges
associated with these SAFETEA-LU provisions. We selected five states in
which to conduct pretests: California, Iowa, Pennsylvania, Utah, and
Washington. In each pretest, we provided a state DOT official with a copy
of our draft survey, asked them to complete it, and then contacted them
after 1 hour to discuss the clarity of each question. Through this method,
we were able to refine the questions and closed-ended responses in our
survey. After the five pretests were completed, we provided a draft copy
of the survey to FHWA and AASHTO for their review and comment. Both
organizations provided technical comments that we incorporated, as
appropriate. Using our professional judgment based on early interviews

with highway project stakeholders and our pretests, we determined that
the survey should be sent to environmental officials at the state DOTs.
However, because the survey considered other aspects of highway
projects—for example planning, right-of-way acquisition, and
construction—language was included in our transmittal e-mails and in the
introduction of the survey to indicate that the state DOT official receiving
our survey should consult with his or her colleagues when completing it.
We felt that it would be far more cumbersome for respondents, and
potentially less reliable, if we were to develop and transmit separate
surveys for each highway project phase—that is, individual surveys that
covered planning, preliminary design and environmental review, final
design and right-of-way acquisition, and construction. Thus, one survey
was developed and respondents were asked to share it and consult with
colleagues when providing responses. We used lists of environmental
officials at the state DOTs that were compiled by AASHTO and the
Transportation Research Board to determine the relevant survey
respondents. The full universe for this survey was 52 state DOTs: all
states, the District of Columbia, and Puerto Rico. We took steps, such as
sending early notification e-mails, to help ensure that the list of
respondents we created was accurate. We launched our survey on
November 30, 2011. We sent e-mail reminders and telephoned survey
respondents who had not completed the survey, urging them to do so as
soon as possible. We eventually received responses from all 52 state
DOTs. We reviewed these responses for inaccuracies or omissions,
analyzed the data, and have presented the key findings in this report. The
survey and its responses—with the exception of open-ended responses
or other identifying information—is reproduced in our e-supplement for
this report: see GAO-12-637SP.

While all state DOTs were included in our survey and, therefore, our data
are not subject to sampling errors, the practical difficulties of conducting
any survey may introduce nonsampling errors. For example, differences
in how a particular question is interpreted, the sources of information
available to respondents, or the types of people who do not respond to a
question can introduce errors into the survey results. We included steps
in both the data collection and data analysis stages to minimize such
nonsampling errors. We collaborated with GAO survey specialists to
design draft questionnaires and, as previously noted, versions of the
questionnaire were pretested, revised, and sent to FHWA and AASHTO
for review and comment. We examined the survey results and performed
computer analyses to identify inconsistencies and other indications of
error and addressed such issues, where possible. A second, independent
analyst checked the accuracy of all computer analyses to minimize the

likelihood of errors in data processing. In addition, GAO analysts
answered respondent questions and resolved difficulties that respondents
had in answering our questions.

To describe the practices state DOTs have implemented on their own to
help expedite highway projects, we included a series of questions in our
survey of state DOTs asking respondents to identify practices they have
implemented in each highway project phase: planning, preliminary design
and environmental review, final design and right-of-way acquisition, and
construction. State DOTs provided these responses in open-ended
questions, which we analyzed. The practices we identified in this report
were those that were cited most frequently by survey respondents. To
collect additional information on efforts both state DOTs and FHWA have
implemented to help expedite highway projects, we reviewed and
analyzed information obtained during the interviews with FHWA (both
headquarters and division offices), state DOTs, and resource agencies.

Appendix II: Initiatives in the Federal Highway Administration's Every Day Counts Effort

The Federal Highway Administration (FHWA) is sharing information on methods to expedite highway projects with state departments of transportation (DOT) through an effort called Every Day Counts. This effort's goals are to shorten project time frames and accelerate technology and innovation by convincing states to adopt proven, rapidly deployable innovations. Under Every Day Counts, FHWA urged state DOTs to consider use of 15 specific initiatives. Every Day Counts promoted the following 10 initiatives to shorten project time frames:

- *Linking planning and environmental review.* This initiative promotes use of planning documents and decisions from the project planning process in the environmental review process. It takes environmental, community, and economic information collected early in the planning stage and carries it through project development, design, and construction. This can lead to decision making that minimizes duplication of effort, promotes environmental stewardship, and reduces delays in project implementation.

- *Early consultation with FHWA environmental attorneys.* Decisions made early in planning and project development are often the root causes of problems identified later in the environmental review process when National Environmental Policy Act of 1969 (NEPA) and Section 4(f) documents undergo legal scrutiny. Consulting with FHWA environmental attorneys at early decision points can help decision makers avoid problems later, saving time and costs.

- *Expanded use of programmatic agreements.* A programmatic agreement is a document that formally spells out the terms of an agreement between a state DOT and other state and/or federal agencies. A programmatic agreement establishes a process for consultation, review, and compliance with one or more federal laws. According to FHWA, programmatic agreements have been effective in producing time savings for completing highway projects.

- *Compensatory mitigation.* The federal Clean Water Act requires compensatory mitigation for projects that cause unavoidable impacts to streams, wetlands, and other waters of the United States. Mitigation for federally protected species may also be required through the Endangered Species Act. Some state laws and regulations also require compensatory mitigation. The permitting process under Section 404 of the Clean Water Act constitutes a major component of the project development and completion process. This initiative proposes expanded use of in-lieu fees and mitigation banking in order to save time and expedite highway projects. See table 5 for information on these compensatory mitigation approaches. Some states have never used mitigation banks or in-lieu fee programs, while others use them for the majority of their mitigation needs.

Table 5: Compensatory Mitigation Approaches Promoted by FHWA's Every Day Counts

Mitigation bank	In-lieu fee program
A mitigation bank is a large-scale mitigation site approved through the federal Clean Water Act and other state programs for resource protection. Each mitigation bank has a formal agreement between the bank sponsor and the Federal regulatory agencies. The agreement details the number of credits the bank can generate; the types of habitat the mitigation bank intends to create, restore, or enhance; and explains the long term management mechanism that will be utilized to ensure the site is protected in perpetuity. In mitigation banking, infrastructure developers buy credits from a bank sponsor before any impacts occur.	An in-lieu fee program conducts wetland, stream, or threatened or endangered species habitat restoration, creation, enhancement, or preservation. In-lieu fee programs may perform various environmental enhancement activities throughout a watershed rather than at one particular site. In-lieu fee programs establish a similar agreement to a mitigation bank agreement, but the sites are not always completely constructed prior to the environmental impacts taking place. Once enough money is received by the program, it implements the project in that watershed. Federal regulations require that in-lieu fee programs be administered by government entities or nonprofits. Users of the program pay a predetermined amount per mitigation credit to a program sponsor, who performs the actual mitigation.

Source: FHWA.

- *Clarifying scope of preliminary design.* Some consider preliminary design to involve only the activities needed to make a NEPA determination; they view everything else as final design activities. This cautious approach delays highway projects because it postpones essential planning until it is too late to be effective. States have the flexibility to pursue many design activities not required for a NEPA determination under preliminary design. When performed concurrently with the NEPA process, these activities can expedite projects without affecting eligibility for federal aid. For example, states can perform soil borings, preliminary traffic control plans, and grading plans.

- *Allowable right-of-way acquisition streamlining.* Before building a highway project, land and property must be acquired by federal, state, and local agencies through right-of-way practices and procedures. Instead of sequentially, these agencies may move elements of a project through the right-of-way process concurrently. This can significantly shorten the highway project development process. To save time, agencies can use these process flexibilities including

- appraisal waiver valuations,

- incentive payments to advance acquisition and relocation, or

- appraisals and negotiations of property acquisition (up to $10,000) by the same individual.

- *Effective coordination for utility relocation.* Approximately half of all highway and bridge projects eligible for federal funding require the relocation or adjustments to accommodate utilities. Gas lines, water lines, waste plumbing, electrical wires, telephone lines, and other wiring are often affected by highway and bridge projects. Flexibilities in place under federal law and regulations foster effective utility coordination during project development by

  - determining the best strategy for physically relocating utilities when needed,

  - documenting the terms and considerations for accomplishing utility relocation activities, and

  - financing the work in an effective and timely manner.

- *FHWA technical assistance for stalled projects.* This initiative focuses on new projects wherein problems are anticipated with conducting an effective project development process, or for "ongoing EISs" where 60 months or more have elapsed since the publishing of the project's notice of intent and no record of decision has been issued. FHWA technical assistance teams will resolve many issues that would otherwise hold up the NEPA review or otherwise delay a project's progress. FHWA subject matter experts can help resolve resource-specific issues concerning wetlands, endangered species, and cultural resources.

- *Use of design-build contracts.* Traditionally, a project is designed, put out for bid to construction firms, then built by the winning bidder (design-bid-build). As discussed above, design-build is an alternate contracting method in which the design and construction phases are combined into one contract, eliminating the separate bid phase and allowing certain aspects of design and construction to take place at the same time. This can provide significant time savings compared with the design-bid-build approach, where the design and construction phases must take place in sequence.

- *Use of construction manager/general contractor contracts.* In a
  construction manager/general contractor project, typically, the owners
  of a project are able to hire a general contractor early in the design
  phase so that the state may benefit from the contractor's
  constructability input as the design develops. This contract type allows
  state DOTs to remain active in the design process while assigning
  risks to the parties most able to mitigate them. This can save time
  because a number of activities can be undertaken concurrently.
  FHWA allows this type of contract only on a trial basis because
  approval is necessary for any nontraditional construction contracting
  technique that deviates from the competitive bidding provisions in
  Section 112 of Title 23 of the U.S. Code.

FHWA promoted five tools to accelerate use of innovative technology,
including three that can shorten the time needed to complete highway
projects:[1]

- *Warm mix asphalt paving.* Warm mix asphalt is the generic term for
  technologies that allow asphalt to be produced and then placed on the
  road at lower temperatures than the conventional hot-mix method. In
  most cases, the lower temperatures result in significant cost savings
  and reduce greenhouse gas emissions because less fuel is required.
  Warm mix asphalt also has the potential to extend the construction
  season, allowing projects to be completed faster.

- *Prefabricated bridge elements.* Use of prefabricated bridge elements
  means that many time-consuming construction tasks no longer need
  to be done sequentially in work zones. An old bridge can be
  demolished while the new bridge elements are built at the same time
  off-site, then brought to the project location ready to erect. Because
  the bridge elements are usually fabricated under controlled climate
  conditions, weather has less impact on the quality, safety, and
  duration of the project. The use of prefabricated bridge elements also
  offers cost savings. The ability to rapidly install prefabricated bridge
  elements on-site can reduce the environmental impact of bridge
  construction in environmentally sensitive areas. See a photograph of
  prefabricated bridge elements being assembled in figure 3.

---

[1]In addition to the innovations that expedite projects, Every Day Counts included two
innovations that serve other purposes—a beveled-edge pavement that improves highway
safety and adaptive signal control technology that reduces travel times and traffic delays.

Figure 3: Prefabricated Bridge Elements at Construction Site

Source: Jerome O'Connor, P.E., BridgeComposites, LLC.

- *Integrated bridge support technology.* Instead of conventional bridge support technology, an innovative bridge system technology uses alternating layers of compacted granular fill material and fabric reinforcement sheets to provide support for the bridge (see fig. 4). The technology, known as geosynthetic reinforced soil technology, offers advantages in the construction of small bridges, including the following:

  - reduced construction time and cost,

  - ease of construction with common equipment and materials,

  - ease of maintenance, and

  - flexible design that is easily modified in the field for unforeseen site conditions.

Figure 4: Geosynthetic Reinforced Soil Technology at a Bridge Construction Site

Source: FHWA.

- *Safety Edge.* The Safety Edge, while not an initiative designed to save time in completing a highway project, is a simple but effective solution that can help save lives by allowing drivers who stray off highways to return to the road safely. Instead of a vertical drop-off, the Safety Edge shapes the edge of the pavement to 30 degrees—the optimal angle to allow drivers to reenter the roadway safely. FHWA's goal is to accelerate the use of the Safety Edge technology, working with states to develop specifications and adopt this pavement edge treatment as a standard practice on all new and resurfacing pavement projects.

- *Adaptive signal control technology.* Poor traffic signal timing contributes to traffic congestion and delay. Conventional signal systems use preprogrammed, daily signal timing schedules. Adaptive signal control technology adjusts the timing of red, yellow and green lights to accommodate changing traffic patterns and ease traffic congestion. Though not designed to save time in completing a highway project, the main benefits of adaptive signal control technology over conventional signal systems are that it can

- continuously distribute green light time equitably for all traffic movements,

- improve travel time reliability by progressively moving vehicles through green lights,

- reduce congestion by creating smoother flow, and

- prolong the effectiveness of traffic signal timing.

Appendix III: GAO Contact and Staff Acknowledgments

GAO Contact	David J. Wise, (202) 512-2834, or wised@gao.gov
Staff Acknowledgments	In addition to the individual named above, Sara Vermillion (Assistant Director); Richard Bulman; Russell Burnett; Richard Calhoon; Steven Elstein; Lorraine Ettaro; Kathleen Gilhooly; Phillip Herr; Richard Johnson; Hannah Laufe; Faye Morrison; Joshua Ormond; Daniel Paepke; and Amy Rosewarne made key contributions to this report.

Please Print on Recycled Paper.

www.ingramcontent.com/pod-product-compliance
Lightning Source LLC
Chambersburg PA
CBHW080911290526
45795CB00007BA/2495